CHRISTMAS TIME IS HERE

7 Arrangements for Brass Quintet

Selections from The Canadian Brass CD
(Opening Day Entertainment Group)

**This Trumpet I part also includes parts for
Piccolo Trumpet and Flugelhorn on some selections.**

ISBN 978-1-4803-6034-1

THE CANADIAN BRASS

DISTRIBUTED BY

HAL•LEONARD®
CORPORATION

7777 W. BLUEMOUND RD. P.O. BOX 13819 MILWAUKEE, WI 53213

www.canadianbrass.com
www.halleonard.com

CONTENTS

Piccolo Trumpet in B♭

ANGEL CHOIR AND THE TRUMPETER

Music and Lyrics by Chris Dedrick
Adapted by Chris Coletti

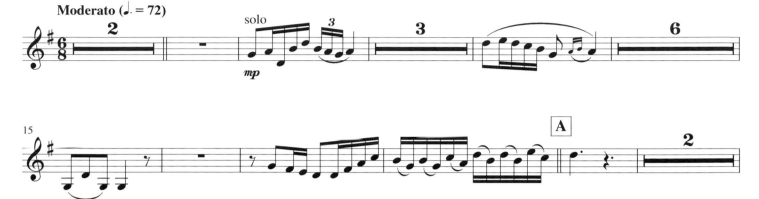

Piccolo Trumpet in B♭

BACH'S BELLS

Inspired by Bach's BWV 29 and
Leontovych's CAROL OF THE BELLS

Chris Coletti

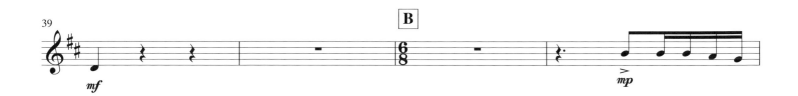

HARK, THE HERALD ANGELS SING

Felix Mendelssohn
Arranged by Brandon Ridenour

8

Trumpet I in B♭

MY LITTLE DRUM

By Vince Guaraldi
Arranged and adapted by Brandon Ridenour

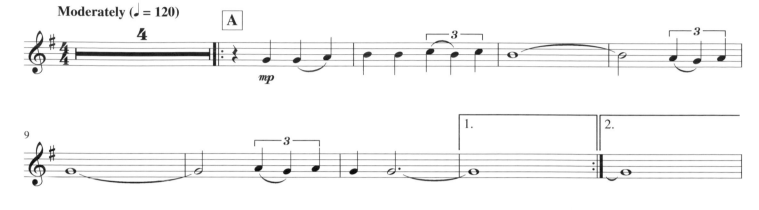

Piccolo Trumpet in B♭

SKATING

By Vince Guaraldi
Arranged by Brandon Ridenour

Bright Jazz Waltz (♩ = 180–200)

Trumpet I in B♭

O TANNENBAUM

Traditional
Arranged by Vince Guaraldi
Adapted by Brandon Ridenour

WHAT CHILD IS THIS?

Traditional
Arranged and adapted by Brandon Ridenour

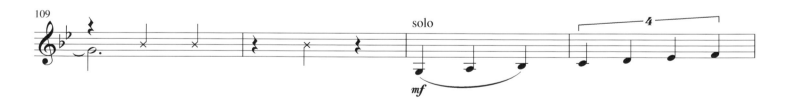